~ THE ~
HIDDEN PAST

Peter Hicks

RSVP
RAINTREE STECK-VAUGHN
P U B L I S H E R S
The Steck-Vaughn Company

Austin, Texas

Published by Raintree Steck-Vaughn Publishers, an imprint of Steck-Vaughn Company

Library of Congress Cataloging-in-Publication Data
Hicks, Peter.
The Hidden Past / Peter Hicks.
    p.   cm.—(Remarkable world)
Includes bibliographical references and index.
Summary: Explains how records of life become hidden and the efforts people have made to reconstruct past civilizations by examining their artifacts, caves, shipwrecks, and burial sites.
ISBN 0-8172-4541-3
1. Archaeology—Juvenile literature.
2. Civilization, Ancient—Juvenile literature.
3. Antiquities—Juvenile literature.
[1. Archaeology. 2. Civilization, ancient.
3. Antiquities.]
I. Title. II. Series.
CC171.H52 1997
930.1—dc20   96-32761

Printed in Italy. Bound in the United States
1 2 3 4 5 6 7 8 9 0 01 00 99 98 97

Picture acknowledgments
AKG 36t; Ancient Art and Architecture Collection 25t; James Davis Photography 12b, 15, 25b, CM Dixon *front cover* right, *front cover* bottom left, 6, 7, 14t, 14b, 19, 26, 29b; ET Archive *front cover* center left, 22-3, 31; Mary Evans Picture Library 9, 32t; Eye Ubiquitous Title page/EJB Hawkins, 20b/L Fordyce, 22b/EJB Hawkins; Robert Harding 10, 11, 12t; Andrew Hasson 33t; Hulton Deutsch 35; Illustrated London News Picture Library 27, 28, 33b; Brian Kooyman, Dept of Archaeology, University of Calgary 8l, 8b; London Transport Museum 36b, 37; Mary Rose Trust 42, 43b, 44t; Peter Newark's Pictures 20t, 23b, 29t, 44b, 45t; Photri 18-19; Rex Features 13/Mauro Carraro, 43t; SNS Pressebild 4b, 5t, 5b; Frank Spooner Pictures 38; Thames Water 34–35; Western Australian Maritime Museum 39t/Peabody Museum of Salem, 39b, 40, 41t 41c, 41b; Woods Hole Oceanographic Institution 45c/Quest Group Ltd. 45b/National Geographic Society/Joseph H. Bailey. Artwork by Peter Bull.

CONTENTS

How the Past Becomes Hidden   **4**

How Ancient Peoples Buried
their Dead   **9**

Finding Lost Cities   **20**

Caves and Tunnels   **26**

How Shipwrecks are Recovered   **39**

Time Line   **46**

Glossary   **47**

Further Information   **47**

Index   **48**

HOW THE PAST BECOMES HIDDEN

Ice-Man found

ONE way we learn about the past is by finding it. Bodies, artifacts, buildings, or a whole civilization can lie undisturbed for many centuries until, by accident or deliberate searching, they are discovered. Such discoveries may answer many important questions or provide clues to past cultures and people's lives. It is a never-ending quest to find out what happened before our time. But how does the past become hidden in the first place?

Ancient civilizations and peoples buried their dead in all kinds of ways, and archaeologists have discovered a great deal from burial sites. However, when a body is buried by accident, finding it again is quite unexpected.

On Thursday September 19, 1991, two climbers in the Otztal Alps of Austria were shocked to find a body sticking out

The Ice-Man, just after his body had been cut from the glacier. He was 5 ft. 3 in. tall and probably between 35 and 40 years old when he died. So far, archaeologists have found 13 tattoos on his back and legs.

The Ice-Man lived in what is known as the Neolithic or "New Stone Age." His people were farmers, who cleared the forested valleys with their axes, grew cereals, peas, oil crops such as linseed, and kept animals. They gathered crab apples, hazelnuts, raspberries, blackberries, and rose hips.

of a glacier (a very slow moving river of ice). "From a distance of twenty-five or thirty feet we suddenly saw something brown sticking out of the ice. Our first thought was that it was trash, perhaps a doll...as we came closer, Erika said, 'But it's a man!'"

The Ice-Man's head. His teeth showed no evidence of decay, but they were quite badly worn due to a diet of hard, dried meat and cereals. The teeth were damaged because the cereals were ground into flour using sandstone grindstones, and pieces of grit found their way into the bread.

The objects that were found on and around the body were carefully taken from the ice and examined. The evidence suggested that this could not have been the victim of a recent climbing accident.

The dead man owned an ax with a copper blade and a flint knife, which seemed to belong to ancient times, such as the Neolithic or Bronze Ages. A series of radiocarbon datings put the date of the man's death at between 3300 and 3200 B.C.—making him over five thousand years old! As the scientists examined the body, they pieced together what they think happened to the "Ice-Man."

He may have been involved in a fight and escaped over the mountains. Wounded and tired, he was engulfed by a terrible blizzard. He slumped down by a rock, fell asleep, and never woke up.

The Ice-Man's ax. It is two feet long and consists of a yew wood handle and a leather binding to hold the copper blade in position.

He was gradually covered by snow and ice, and then lay undisturbed for five thousand years. Archaeologists have learned a tremendous amount about his clothing and the objects he was carrying. His equipment was impressive: a bow and arrows, a backpack, as well as flint and bone tools contained in a belt pouch. His fur clothes, cap, and

Hidden artifacts

Our knowledge of warfare before the development of writing comes almost totally from archaeology. Although weapons and armor have been found in burial chambers, some are in unusual places. The Celts of Europe hurled precious shields, helmets, and swords into rivers, sometimes damaging them first. They were probably offerings, or gifts, to their gods who were believed to live in water. Many hoards of bronze axes and other tools have been found in fields, ditches, or near local landmarks. It is believed that Celtic bronzesmiths hid them in times of emergency, or for safety, or simply to store them, since bronze was very valuable at that time. What we will probably never know is why no one ever retrieved them.

This hoard of Celtic coins was found in Bavaria, Germany. When discovered, these hoards are very helpful to archaeologists in understanding where the coins were minted and over what distance coins were traded.

cloak were all designed to keep out the cold. His shoes even had grass stuffing to trap heat. The Saami (Lapps), who live in the far north of Europe, still do this to keep their feet warm.

There are many civilizations of the past that were wiped out by disease, famine, or more powerful peoples. Some of their lost cities have been discovered, such as those of the Mayans in Central America. The jungle completely covered the Mayan ruins for centuries until intrepid explorers set out to find them. There is also a wealth of hidden past at the bottom of the oceans that sometimes needs the most up-to-date technology to discover. Ships on the high seas, sometimes with incredible treasures in their holds, have sunk after being struck by a storm, or had holes torn in their hulls on rocks and barrier reefs. One great ship, the *Titanic*, hit an iceberg and sank in 1912 on her maiden voyage. Other great vessels have been sunk in times of war, such as the battleship *Bismarck*, the pride of Adolf Hitler's German navy in World War II.

A superb iron dagger and bronze sheath dating from the fifth or sixth century B.C. The fine craftsmanship suggests they were made for an aristocratic warrior, because such a weapon could only have been afforded by a very wealthy person.

Bison bones excavated at Head-Smashed-In Buffalo Jump, Alberta, Canada. The layer of bones there is over 30 ft. deep. Archaeologists believe that the site was first used almost 8,000 years ago and may have been abandoned as recently as 250 years ago.

Between 12,000 and 6,000 years ago, a group known as the Palaeo-Indians lived in North America. They survived by hunting large animals, such as mammoths, mastodons, ground sloths, and bison.

The Palaeo-Indian hunters killed these creatures on a massive scale. They were nomadic people who followed the animals on their seasonal migrations. From evidence that has been found by archaeologists, we know that in about 8000 B.C., near Casper, Wyoming, a group of 15 to 20 hunters trapped and killed 75 bison. They then butchered them on the spot, stripping about 19 tons of meat from the carcasses. At other sites, such as Olsen-Chubbuck, Colorado, and Head-Smashed-In Buffalo Jump, Canada, herds of bison were killed by being stampeded over a cliff into a gully.

Below The bison-kill site at Head-Smashed-In Buffalo Jump was used by the Blackfoot Native Americans. A herd of bison was frightened, stampeded, and guided toward the edge of a cliff, 60 feet high. They were either killed outright by the fall or were shot at the foot of the cliff with spears and arrows.

HOW ANCIENT PEOPLE BURIED THEIR DEAD

IN 113 B.C., Prince Liu Sheng of China died. He had been the ruler of the important Chung-Shan state near Beijing. He was a harsh ruler, who enjoyed drinking and feasting while his people starved and were made homeless by terrible floods. In 104 B.C., his wife, Dou Wan, died and was buried in a cavern adjoining the place where Liu Sheng's body lay.

A royal burial

For both funerals, each body was taken to the rocky hills near the town of Man-ch'eng, in Hebei Province. They were buried in two huge caverns carved by slaves from solid rock, along with offerings and artifacts. They were then sealed in with huge boulders and molten iron to protect them from grave robbers. The bodies of Liu Sheng and his wife were never again to see the light of day.

One night in June 1968, a group of soldiers from the Chinese army were on patrol. In the dark, two of them tripped and fell into a hole, which on closer examination seemed to lead underground.

Liu Sheng was appointed ruler of Chung-Shan by his brother, the Emperor Wu-ti in 153 B.C.

Their officer led them through a narrow channel, which suddenly opened into a huge chamber. The soldiers could not believe their eyes as their torches lit up gold, silver, and jade ornaments, and rows and rows of clay and bronze pots. Immediately, the soldiers posted guards on the entrance and told the authorities of their find. Archaeologists from Beijing soon arrived and, by carefully studying the inscriptions in the chamber, discovered that the tomb's ancient occupant was Prince Liu Sheng. One of the most sensational finds of all time had been made completely by accident.

The prince lives again

Outside, more soldiers were scouring the nearby hillsides to see if there were other hidden tombs. One hill was covered with fine, loose rock, that hid another entrance. This one was sealed with a solid stone wall, and the blocks were bonded together with molten iron. Army engineers were called in to blast a way through—as carefully as possible. When the dust settled, they found themselves in the tomb of Dou Wan, Liu Sheng's wife.

The contents of the tombs were so vast that it took the archaeologists, helped by the army, over two months to survey and record the chambers and remove the artifacts. In all, there were over 2,800 of them. Chinese nobles

One of a set of four beautiful bronze leopards decorated with silver and garnet (a semiprecious stone) from Dou Wan's tomb. It is thought they were used to weigh down the corners of the funeral pall (a cloth that covered the coffin).

obviously believed that they could take their possessions with them to their next life, because the quality of the gold and silver vases, ornaments, lacquerwork, and silks was superb. There were incense burners, leopard statues, and sets of clay figures. One clay tray found in Dou Wan's tomb had designs of acrobats, musicians, dancers, and a contortionist on it to keep the Princess amused in the afterlife.

Suits of jade

Probably the most spectacular finds in the tombs were the superb yu-xia, or jade suits, which contained the bodies of Liu Sheng and Dou Wan. It was common for royalty to be buried in these splendid suits, believing that jade would preserve their bodies for the afterlife. Each suit was made with about two thousand small jade plaques, divided into eight sections, and sewn together with gold thread.

Unfortunately, as the bodies decomposed, the suits collapsed. When Liu Sheng's suit was removed, all that was left of him were his teeth.

Liu Sheng's wonderful jade suit consisted of boots, trousers, armlets, gloves, upper vest, helmet, and mask. All of the pieces were tailored to fit perfectly.

An artist's impression of how the terra-cotta army might have looked when new and freshly painted. The carriages and horses were made of cast bronze pieces that were welded together. It is believed that once the bronzesmiths had finished their work, they were executed and buried, taking the secrets of Shi Huang Di's tomb to their graves.

Guarding the dead

Another accident led to the discovery of an even more famous Chinese burial. In 1974, a group of farmers in Xian province were digging a well near the burial mound of Emperor Qin Shi Huang Di, who had ruled from 246 to 210 B.C. They dug into a huge, underground pit and found six thousand life-sized warriors made of terracotta, a kind of pottery similar to that used in flower pots. The warriors were all in military formation. Each one was six feet tall, had its correct rank displayed on its armor, and had unique facial features. In 1976, two more pits were discovered. The larger pit contained 1,400 warriors and horses, and the smaller pit contained only 68 warriors. It is believed that when they were made, over two thousand years ago, each warrior had been carefully painted. They must have been a wonderful sight, standing straight in their ranks before they were buried.

A close-up of one of the terra-cotta warriors

The man who was responsible for this extraordinary show of wealth—Qin Shi Huang Di—became emperor when he was only 13. By 221 B.C., when he was 38, he had conquered most of China. He made plans for his death as soon as he took the throne, and 700,000 laborers were forced to work on his tomb for 36 years before it was ready. The massive army he assembled around his burial mound was probably intended to protect him in the afterlife. To construct the burial chamber, the laborers had to dig through three subterranean streams, which they sealed off with bronze. They built models of palaces, pavilions, and offices, and filled the tomb with fine vessels, precious stones, and rare objects. Artisans were ordered to install mechanically triggered crossbows set to shoot any intruder.

The terra-cotta statues have taught archaeologists a great deal about military armor and uniforms in ancient China.

PRECTECTVS CESQVET
IN PACE VIXIT ANNIS
MENSES
NVTRICATVS DEO CRISTO

Above The early Christians carved inscriptions above the burial chambers to commemorate those who had died, often giving their age. This inscription "prays" that the person "rests in peace and finds comfort in Christ…."

Right This statue shows Christ as the Good Shepherd saving a lost sheep. To early Christians, on their own in a hostile world, images like this must have been comforting.

The underground world of the dead

Under the city of Rome, Italy, lie 42 incredible honeycomb-like structures— the catacombs, or underground cemeteries. The catacombs are complicated burial chambers and passages, hollowed out of the soft rock beneath the city. They were built by professional diggers called *fossores*, who cut passages into the sides of hills. Spaces were dug for up to three people along the passages. Some chambers were big enough to hold entire families. The entrances to the chambers were often beautifully painted, and many carried carvings and inscriptions. These amazing structures were built for a simple reason.

The catacombs date mainly from the third century A.D., when Christians in the

14

Right Sicilians visited their mummified relatives regularly. They often talked to them, keeping them up to date on the latest news and asking for advice on family problems. This was not thought of as unusual, but as a way to keep in touch with their dead ancestors. Today, the catacombs are very popular with tourists.

Roman Empire were persecuted because they refused to accept that the Emperor was a god. Many Christian cemeteries were destroyed, and the Emperor Valerian forbade Christians even to visit cemeteries. The Christians needed safer and more secret burial places, so they built the catacombs.

In the centuries after the fall of Rome in A.D. 395, the catacombs were forgotten. It was not until the sixteenth century that people began to search for them. Exploring them was quite dangerous. Many unsuspecting visitors were injured or even killed by cave-ins. The staircases that linked the different passages were very steep and dangerous.

The forgotten mummies of Palermo

In the nineteenth century, the ground beneath other cities was explored. Naples, Tunis, Sicily, and Malta were also discovered to have catacombs. In fact, the catacombs of Palermo, Sicily, were found to contain over six thousand mummies! About four hundred years ago, it was very popular among Palermo's professional people, such as doctors and lawyers, to have their bodies preserved after they died. This tradition was carried on until 1920, when the last person to be mummified and placed in the catacombs was the 2-year-old daughter of a doctor.

The extraordinarily neat stacks of leg bones and skulls in the Paris catacombs. What was once considered a health hazard became an attraction for both Parisians and tourists alike.

Piles of bones under Paris

Hidden deep below the streets of Paris is a maze of underground mines, once used as stone quarries for the city's many buildings. Dark, damp, and mysterious, they were perfect hiding places for thieves and criminals on the run. As a joke, the Parisians called them the catacombs, after the catacombs in Rome. The joke became reality when the mines actually did become a resting place for the dead.

In the 1780s, many wealthy Parisians were very worried about the huge cemeteries in the city, as they thought the smells from the rotting corpses contained poisonous fumes. The authorities ordered the destruction of the biggest, and smelliest— the Cimetière des Innocents. For nearly two years from December 1785, workmen dug up the corpses and transported their remains by horse and cart into the catacombs.

Wealthy, fashionable Parisians in 1897 at a concert in the catacombs. Events like this were the talk of the town and were very well attended.

Death among the bones

In 1871, the Paris catacombs witnessed a truly dreadful event. The year before, in 1870, the French had been defeated by the Prussians in the Franco-Prussian War. The Paris Commune, a group of Parisian Republicans, tried to govern Paris. They challenged the newly formed French government in Versailles, led by Louis Adolphe Thiers. However, Thiers was determined not to allow these revolutionaries, known as the Communards, to overthrow him, and sent the army to hunt them down. After terrible bloodshed on both sides, some Communards fled to the catacombs and hid from the government troops. They were safe for a short time, but the soldiers eventually broke in at two different points, cornered the ringleaders among the skeletons, and gunned them down. The uprising was over quickly.

A French officer watches the Communards fleeing into the catacombs, while his men reload their rifles for the final attack.

This grisly task continued well into the nineteenth century, when other cemeteries were also destroyed. The skeletons, once deposited, were carefully stacked into piles and patterns of skulls, ribs, arm and leg bones. Today, it is still possible to go and visit these remains of an estimated six million Parisians.

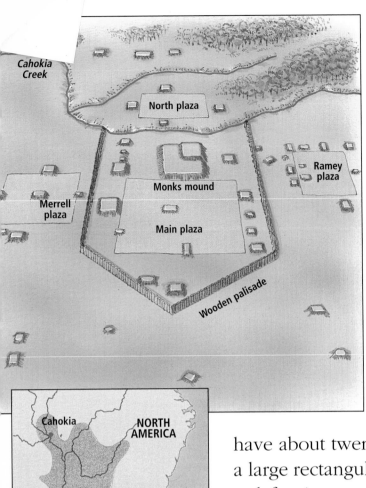

Cahokia Creek

North plaza

Monks mound

Ramey plaza

Merrell plaza

Main plaza

Wooden palisade

Cahokia

NORTH AMERICA

Moundville

Top Cahokia contained over 100 earth mounds. The largest is more than 100 ft. high.
Inset map The Mississippian people lived in the fertile valleys of the Ohio, Mississippi, Tennessee, and Missouri rivers.

The temple-mounds of Mississippi

The first real towns in North America appeared about A.D. 700 in the middle Mississippi Valley of what is now the United States. They usually consisted of a group of flat-topped, rectangular mounds, with temples, timber homes, and mortuary houses built on top. A town center would have about twenty mounds grouped around a large rectangular plaza and be enclosed by a defensive wooden stockade. These towns served two main purposes. They were centers where food and materials were collected and distributed, and places where ceremonies were held.

One of these towns, called Cahokia, was in a large fertile valley close to where the Missisippi, Missouri, and Illinois rivers meet. It had more than a hundred mounds and housed a population of

Below A burial chamber excavated at Moundville, Alabama. The jars and bowls probably contained food and drink to help the dead on their journey to the afterlife.

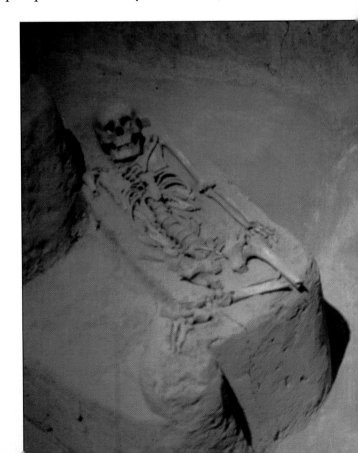

about ten thousand people. It became the main town of the communities that grew up in the area.

As with many cultures, there were set rituals for burying the dead. The most important people were usually laid out on wooden stretchers in the mortuary houses. Other corpses were first decomposed in charnel houses, and the bundles of bones were then given a second elaborate burial in the mounds. Snail or conch shells, pearls, seashells, and embossed copper sheets were often buried with them. Servants were sometimes killed and buried with their masters.

In about A.D. 1450 in the area around Cahokia, the populations were all but wiped out, probably by tuberculosis or internal parasites caused by overcrowding and poor sanitation. European explorers and settlers who arrived in the sixteenth century brought diseases with them that killed many of the inhabitants of the temple-mounds.

In some mounds, archaeologists have found evidence of a religion called the Southern Cult that reached its peak in A.D. 1250. This figure of a man was excavated at Spiro in what is now Oklahoma.

FINDING LOST CITIES

THE great Mayan civilization of Central America flourished for over a thousand years in the Yucatán peninsula of Mexico and parts of Guatemala and Honduras. From the second century B.C., the Maya built many vast temple-cities with splendid buildings, statues, carvings, and paintings, and they devised their own system of hieroglyphic writing. Some of their cities were abandoned in the ninth and early tenth centuries. The Mayan civilization was finally destroyed by Spanish invaders in 1697. Their wonderful, abandoned cities were engulfed by the thick, lush jungle that grows in the region. In just a few years, some of the greatest archaeological treasures of the area were hidden by dense undergrowth.

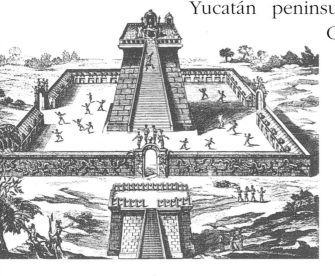

This fanciful eighteenth-century picture is a reconstruction of how the temples of Central America looked before they were claimed by the dense jungle. Bloodthirsty accounts of human sacrifices were very popular at that time.

The ruined city of Uxmal in the northeastern Yucatán. This dramatic photograph shows how easily the thick jungle covers the remains of a once-great city. Only the huge wall remains visible.

Secrets of the jungle

In the 1780s, the Spanish government in Guatemala heard reports of mysterious ruins in the jungle. In 1786, they sent an army captain, Antonio del Rio, to investigate. He took an artist, Ricardo Almendariz, to sketch anything important. After many hazardous months of cutting their way through thick jungle, they found an impressive group of stone buildings, totally covered in undergrowth. They had stumbled upon the Mayan city of Palenque, which was built in A.D. 642. On their return, they wrote a report, which was filed away and forgotten. Although other explorers found Mayan ruins, their whereabouts were known only to a small number of people.

The dramatic expeditions of the American explorer John Lloyd Stephens and British explorer Frederick Catherwood, in 1839–42, brought the wonders of the Mayan ruins to the world's notice. Stephens was appointed U.S. ambassador to Central America giving him some protection from the dangers of the region, mainly the political instability. Starting out from Belize, the pair searched for Copán, a great Mayan city in what is now Honduras.

GULF OF MEXICO

Mérida
Chichén Itzá
Uxmal
YUCATÁN PENINSULA
Palenque
Tikal
MEXICO
Copán
Kaminaljuyú

A map of the Yucatán peninsula and the location of the rediscovered Mayan cities

The impressive palace and tower in the ruins of Palenque, southern Yucatán. The palace was a huge maze of galleries, rooms, courtyards, and patios. It is dominated by the four-story square tower, which could have been an observatory or a watchtower.

After reaching the modern village of Copán, they set out into the jungle. Hacking their way through thick foliage and journeying upward (Copán is 2,100 feet above sea level), they came upon a city wall, overgrown with vines and other plants. They entered the city, and were amazed by what they found—fine buildings, temple pyramids, and wide squares. Stephens wrote: "The City was desolate.... It lay before us like a shattered bark in the midst of the ocean, her masts gone, her name effaced, her crew perished, and none to tell whence she came, to whom she belonged, how long on her voyage, or what caused her destruction." The jungle was so dense that, at first, Catherwood did not have enough light to draw his pictures properly, so the men hired workers to cut away the forest.

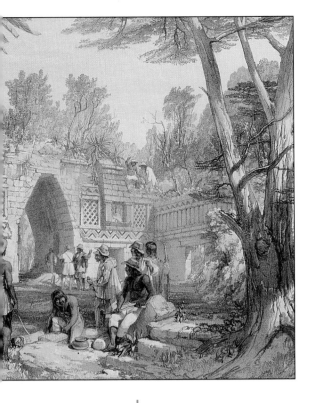

After bargaining with the landowner, Stephens was able to buy the ruins for $50. This allowed Catherwood to explore them thoroughly and make very detailed drawings.

The next year the two explorers reached Palenque. Although it was totally hidden in dense foliage, they found two impressive temples and a palace. Pushing north, they reached Uxmal in the Yucatán, with its huge palace, ball court, and temple pyramid. At this point, Catherwood was struck down with a serious bout of malaria, and the pair had to return to New York. Stephens published his account of their adventures in *Incidents of Travel in Central America, Chiapas and Yucatán*, illustrated by Catherwood. With later accounts of their journeys to Chichén Itzá and Tulum, the pair caused a sensation. They helped to begin the great age of Mayan archaeology.

A carved "stele," or pillar, drawn by Catherwood. Mayan designs were so unusual and complicated that he had trouble drawing them at first.

Above One of Frederick Catherwood's pictures of his explorations in the Yucatán

The secret well at Chichén Itzá

Chichén Itzá means "wells of the Itzá." The city is in an area that lacks rivers, but the rainfall filters through the limestone rock to form huge natural wells called cenotes. Chichén Itzá was sited near two such cenotes.

Underwater archaeology does not always take place at sea. Edward Thompson, an American explorer and archaeologist, was inspired by John Lloyd Stephens's writings on Mayan cities. Thompson was fascinated by the story of the Sacred Well, or cenote, at Chichén Itzá, into which, according to legend, human sacrifices and precious stones were thrown in times of drought. In 1885, he visited the well, which was a huge, naturally formed hole in the limestone rock, full of deep water. It had a diameter of 200 feet and an 80-foot drop to the water. Thompson learned deep-sea diving, and employed two Greek sponge fishermen to help explore the well. In 1904, he also brought a huge dredger to help search the well.

At first he found nothing. He was on the brink of despair when, suddenly, his

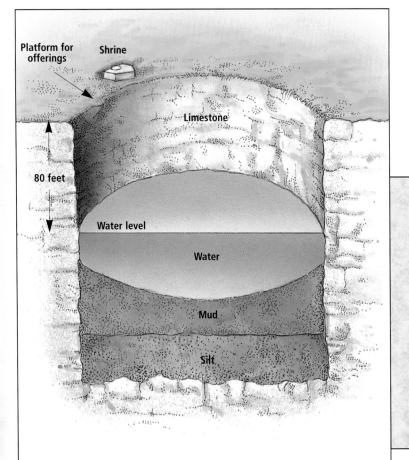

Platform for offerings
Shrine
Limestone
80 feet
Water level
Water
Mud
Silt

Danger in the well

"Every little while one of the stone blocks, loosened from its place in the wall...would come plunging down upon us.... Had we been incautiously standing with our backs to the wall, we should have been sheared in two as if by a pair of gigantic shears."
Edward Thompson describing the dangers of diving in the Sacred Well at Chichén Itzá

A battle scene from the Temple of the Tigers, above the east wall of the Chichén Itzá ball court. Because the details are so convincing, it is believed that the artist must have witnessed fighting between Mayan warriors and neighboring tribes.

luck changed. One day, two strange yellow-white balls were pulled up. Thompson looked at them, broke one in half, and tasted it. He threw a piece onto the fire and it produced sweet-smelling smoke. It was incense, used by the Mayan priests. This encouraged Thompson, and soon the dredger brought up flint and obsidian weapons, ornaments, gold bells, and jade bowls. These finds were important because they showed the wide trade contacts the Mayans had. Finally, human bones were revealed. The legend of human sacrifice was true. Thompson dived to the parts of the well the dredger could not reach. This was dangerous and, although no one was killed, Thompson later became deaf because the huge water pressure from diving in deep water had damaged his ears.

A statue of "chac-mool," or messenger of the gods, from Chichén Itzá. On his stomach is a plate with a gift to the sun.

CAVES AND TUNNELS

ONE popular view of prehistory (the time before history was recorded) is that of cave people—grunting, mindless, and violent—living out their days in damp caves. Certainly, in highland areas, caves were very effective as shelters from the cold and fierce wild animals. However, research has shown that some prehistoric peoples were caring, generous, and creative, despite the harsh world they lived in.

The surprising Neanderthals

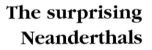

High in the Zagros Mountains of northern Iraq is the huge Shanidar cave, with a gaping entrance 23 feet high and 92 feet wide. There, in the late 1950s, archaeologist Ralph Solecki started searching for evidence of the Neanderthals. The Neanderthals lived in Asia and Europe between

Left Because Neanderthals lived during the last great ice age, they had to cope with the extreme cold. Their large bodies conserved heat and the sinuses in their brow were enlarged in order to warm the freezing air that would otherwise have damaged their lungs.

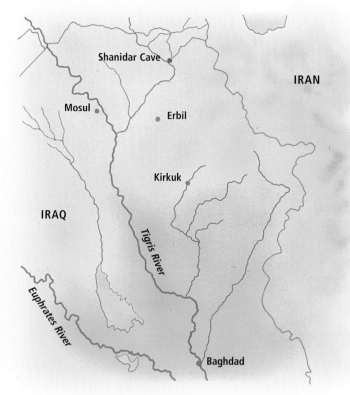

Shanidar Cave

IRAN

Mosul

Erbil

Kirkuk

IRAQ

Tigris River

Euphrates River

Baghdad

Baradost, one of the peaks in the Zagros Mountains, is pierced by many caves. Ralph Solecki was guided to *Shkaft Mazia Shanidar* (Kurdish for "Big Cave Shanidar") after searching 40 different caves in the area.

100,000 and 40,000 years ago. They were similar to modern humans, but had enlarged jaws and brows, and sloping foreheads. Shanidar's floor was mostly made of earth rather than rock, and Solecki thought it was very likely that prehistoric remains would be hidden in the soil. He and his team of workers cut their way through 50 feet of earth and rock.

Their first find was a tiny Neanderthal infant, less than a year old. It seemed likely that adult remains were not far away. In April 1957, Solecki found the badly crushed skull of a Neanderthal man, probably damaged by a rock fall during an earthquake. "The skull looked like a very soiled and broken gigantic egg. A Neanderthal if ever I saw one," said Ralph Solecki. The soil around the skeleton was found to contain pollen from hyacinths, hollyhocks, groundsel (a type of weed), and pine branches.

The skull of the Neanderthal killed by the huge blow to his head. His sloping forehead, heavy brow, and massive jaw can clearly be seen. The front parts of the mouth and jaw were used as a vise to grip meat while it was being butchered.

It appears that the dead man's body had been placed on the pine branches then perhaps covered with flowers—evidence that these Neanderthals felt grief and loss, and conducted funerals just as we do.

Nine skeletons were found in all. One male skeleton showed evidence of physical problems. His right arm was withered and useless, and it had been amputated (cut off) at the elbow. This early surgery had probably been carried out with a sharp flint. His teeth were badly worn, which suggests that he used them, as well as his left arm, to grip and carry things. This person probably could not have hunted, fought, or cared for himself on his own, and he must have been looked after by the group he lived with. This shows that the Neanderthals cared for and supported one another over 40,000 years ago, and were the first humans to bury their dead in graves.

The discovery of the "cared-for" Neanderthal. His skeleton was found by accident when excavations removed a dangerous rock overhang inside the cave.

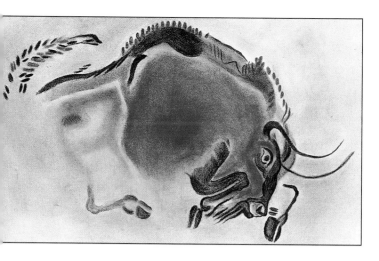

A cave painting of a charging bison. By studying such pictures carefully, archaeologists have found out how they were painted. The shape of the animal was first scraped with a stone, and then outlined in charcoal. The paint—made from ground rocks mixed with water or fat—was applied with the fingers.

Ancient masterpieces

In 1940, in Montignac, southwest France, four boys set about exploring a cave in the woods. They lit their lanterns and scrambled in, one by one, through a hole in the cave's roof. As they pushed their way along the rocky passageway, one of them cried out in amazement. His lantern illuminated the most incredible paintings. Colorful bulls, cows, deer, and horses appeared before them on the white limestone walls of the cave.

These superb, 15,000-year-old art treasures are known as the Lascaux Caves. When the experts came to study the wonderful images, they were amazed at the high levels of skill that these early artists had possessed. Confident outlines, full of movement, showed the animals running and jumping. One group of stags seemed to be crossing a river. Their necks were strained upward, and their noses and branched antlers were held high and proud in the air.

Ever since their discovery, many experts have wondered why so much time and trouble was spent painting these wonderful images.

Scenes like this may have been painted as hunting lessons, to illustrate stories, or simply for pleasure. They may have also been offerings to the gods asking for a plentiful supply of food.

People at that time lived as hunter-gatherers, eating wild vegetables, fruits, nuts, and berries, and hunting animals for meat. They followed herds throughout the year, killing creatures when they needed meat. Bands of hunters used flint-tipped spears and, in rocky areas, made herds stampede over cliffs, killing the injured animals at the bottom. These animals were a crucial part of early man's existence; perhaps the paintings at Lascaux were a way of honoring the animals that kept them alive.

Tunnels

Nowadays, we often forget how important tunnels are. For thousands of years they have been built for transportation and to take away unpleasant things, including human sewage. The disposal of sewage has been a major problem throughout history. Even in the newly industrialized cities of nineteenth-century Europe, sewage was still a major problem. It led to the terrible epidemics of diseases like cholera. In London, England, the problem was particularly bad, with the Thames River being both the city's main water supply and its main sewer! Something had to be done.

The world's first sewers?

Although tunnels are technically very difficult to build, the Indus Valley civilization (2500–1500 B.C.) had a very good drainage system—especially at Mohenjo-Daro, in what is now Pakistan—complete with manholes at regular intervals. Many of the streets had drains with baked brick roofs, and the contents of baths and toilets were discharged into them from individual houses.

Main picture The impressive remains of Mohenjo-Daro, excavated during the 1920s. On the high ground, the tower of the citadel—the fortress that protected the city—can be seen clearly.

Inset A plan of the excavated areas of Mohenjo-Daro

North

Main streets with brick-built drains

Citadel

Plan of excavated areas of Mohenjo-Daro

0   200 m

0   200 yards

How London's underground sewage system was built. The city's roads were closed off and dug up, and armies of workers were sent in to build the brick tunnels. When complete, the tunnels were simply covered again with soil and the road surface.

The Great Stink of 1858

The story of Great Britain's first underground sewage system actually began with the terrible smell of the Thames River.

In the nineteeth century, as most of London's sewage ended up in the Thames, the smell in the summertime was awful. On June 30, 1858—which was a very hot day—an important committee meeting was taking place in the Houses of Parliament, directly overlooking the river. At that time, it was believed that the disease cholera could be caught by breathing in the smell, or miasma, of raw sewage. *The Times* newspaper reported that Benjamin Disraeli, the Chancellor of the Exchequer, rushed from the foul-smelling committee room with a handkerchief held tightly to his nose. He was followed by another equally panic-stricken politician, William Gladstone. So bad was the "Great Stink"—as the summer of 1858 became known—that the bill to build an underground sewage system was put before Parliament within two weeks, and it became law after another three. As most bills took months, or even years, to become law, this was remarkable.

Below A cross-section of Bazalgette's embankment beneath Charing Cross Station. The tunnels contain gas and water (1), the low-level sewer (2), and the Metropolitan underground railroad (3). The people on the embankment are unaware of what is underneath!

32

Right This beam engine pumped thousands of gallons of water a day from a well over 100 feet underground. The water was flushed into sewers and pipes.

Joseph Bazalgette

In the 1860s, engineer Joseph Bazalgette designed a system of tunnels to divert rivers into lagoons downstream from the city before they deposited their loads of human waste in the Thames River. Huge steam engines inside water pumping stations were used to pump millions of gallons of water up from below-ground to help flush the sewage down the tunnels into the lagoons. Bazalgette's sewer system was copied in many other cities in Great Britain, including Birmingham and Liverpool, as well as many major cities in Europe and the United States.

His work was a great contribution to modern civilization, although it is totally hidden from view. The original system in London still works today, and consists of 80 miles of sewer tunnels under the city's streets, built with 318 million bricks and capable of carrying about 500 million gallons of sewage a day.

Many old sewer tunnels are still working well, but they need constant care and maintenance. This is because heavy traffic on the roads above places a huge strain on the brickwork.

Down below

The objects that you find, down below,
Help to entertain the mind down below,
There are watches you can't wind
Wrapped up in bacon rind
And that isn't all you find, down below.

O there's something in a sewer, down below,
That has a strange allure, down below,
And the magic of the drain
Is something I can't explain,
But it's calling me again, down below.

Sung in Victorian Music Halls, England

Plotting in the sewers

Just as London built a proper sewage system in the 1860s, so too did Paris. By 1911, the city had 753 miles of sewers. As a result of the improved sanitation, the disease cholera became much less common than before.

With this sewer labyrinth and the catacombs under its streets, perhaps it is not surprising that sometimes secret or illegal groups used these ready-made underground hideouts below the French capital.

One of the strangest groups to use them was formed in the 1930s and was known as the Cagoules, or hoods. They were a Fascist organization opposed to democracy, and under their leader, Eugène Deloncle, obtained detailed plans of the sewers and catacombs of Paris. There the Cagoules built headquarters, stores, and even prison cells, and equipped themselves with weapons to attack their enemies from underground.

Crowds watch as the Paris police carry away rifles and machine guns belonging to the Cagoules in 1937. With their detailed maps and plans of the sewers, it was easy for the Cagoules to hide their weapons.

Above This cross section underneath a Paris street shows the opportunities illegal groups had for operating in the sewers and catacombs.

Some of the Cagoules' strange ideas involved trying to convert refuse carts into armored cars, and they even attempted to steal the deadly germ botulism from the Pasteur Institute to infect ex-Cagoule members who had joined a rival organization. The Cagoules were one of France's least successful political groups.

During one of the darkest periods in French history—the German occupation between 1940 and 1944 in World War II—the sewers had a role to play again. First, the Germans used them as air raid shelters from Allied bombings. Afraid they might be attacked by the French when they were

sheltering, the Germans constructed 300 barbed wire barriers for protection. Toward the end of the occupation, the French Resistance groups—fighting for their freedom against the Germans—built headquarters in both the sewers and the catacombs. They prepared to use the sewer telephone system in case the Germans destroyed the overground telephones, cutting off communication. If the lines in the sewers were cut, it was arranged for the 250 sewermen to carry messages swiftly to all parts of the city. When the fighting broke out between the Resistance and the retreating Germans, manholes made excellent places to attack from or retreat to, and the Resistance based their first-aid stations in the sewers under the Rue Gay Lussac.

The end of the line

The underground railroad system beneath London, England, is bigger than it appears on maps. Over the years, some parts of the system have fallen into disuse and have been abandoned. Underneath the streets of London lie ghost stations where trains no longer stop and where passengers no longer wait.

The platform (**left**) and a section of tunnel (**right**) at King William Street Station near the Bank of England, London. The station closed on February 24, 1900, and is now deserted and neglected.

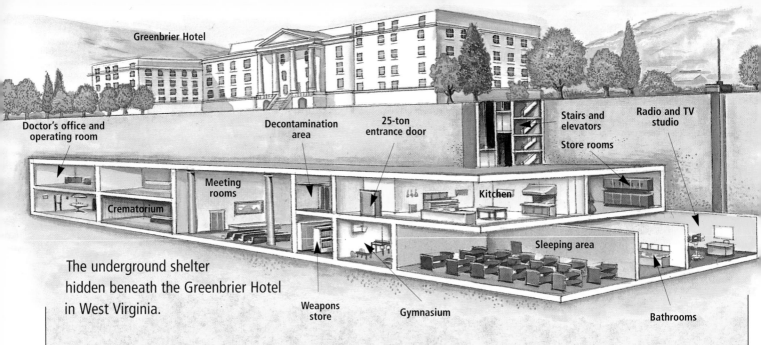

Greenbrier Hotel

Doctor's office and operating room

Decontamination area

25-ton entrance door

Stairs and elevators

Radio and TV studio

Store rooms

Meeting rooms

Crematorium

Kitchen

Sleeping area

The underground shelter hidden beneath the Greenbrier Hotel in West Virginia.

Weapons store

Gymnasium

Bathrooms

Secret hideouts of the Superpowers

In 1959, a large new wing was built on one of the United States most exclusive hotels—the Greenbrier, near White Sulphur Springs, in West Virginia. No one guessed that this was simply a cover to hide the construction of a top secret underground bunker 65 feet below it.

The bunker was designed as a refuge where the president and senior members of the government could survive for two months underground. The plan, called Project Greek Island, was General Eisenhower's idea. He was then president of the United States, and he wanted to be prepared for a possible nuclear war with the Soviet Union.

The bunker had one thousand bunk beds in dormitories, a small hospital, a TV studio, a weapons store, and a crematorium. There were no luxuries—just the bare necessities to survive. The bunker remained a well-kept secret until it was discovered by a journalist in 1992.

The Americans were not the only people to build such shelters. With the weakening of the Communist government in the Soviet Union during the late 1980s, stories reached the West about a huge labyrinth hundreds of feet below Moscow. Built by the KGB, the former Soviet Union's secret police, it was designed to enable the Soviet government to carry on in the event of a war with the West. Because it was so deep underground and was equipped with its own life-support system, this reinforced concrete city could withstand chemical, biological, and even nuclear attacks. It contained vast supplies of food and water, cafeterias, sleeping quarters, and hospital units. Even today, the exact size and layout of the underground city is a mystery.

Beneath this building in Moscow, Russia, lies a maze of tunnels running in all directions. One leads to the Kremlin, and another contains a railroad line leading to the airport that was used by the leaders of the Soviet Union.

HOW SHIPWRECKS ARE RECOVERED

A diver recovering coins carefully from the ocean bed off Point Cloates, Western Australia. When experts examined them, they found the vast majority were Spanish dollars.

IN 1811, a merchant ship was sailing its usual route across the Indian Ocean to Canton, China, carrying gold, silver, and ballast (stone to stabilize the ship, which would be replaced in Canton with valuable pepper). The ship was heading for Point Cloates on the west coast of Australia. The waters it was sailing through were treacherous, containing uncharted coral reefs and jagged rocks. Suddenly a storm blew up, and the ship was driven toward the deadly obstacles. Seeing the disaster coming, most of the crew safely abandoned ship, but the vessel was holed and sank to the seabed. It settled on its port (left) side, which became covered with silt. The starboard (right) side gradually rotted away. The ocean had claimed another ship.

In 1974, a group of divers swimming off Point Cloates, a remote area on the west coast of Australia, discovered the wreck of a ship, its hull half-buried in the sand.

In the days of sailing ships, shipwrecks were very common. In bad weather it was fairly easy for a ship to drift or be blown onto rocks or run aground. The life of a sailor was hazardous, and many perished on the seas.

The ship's bell, some coins, and a broken pottery flagon (bottle). The flagon probably contained wine. Alcohol was common on board sailing ships: wine or beer was safer to drink than water, which quickly went bad.

This is a treacherous part of the Australian coastline, and many ships had been wrecked on its rocky reefs and jagged cliffs. Swimming carefully around the wreck, divers noticed spilled ballast stone and a scattering of coins. Within a few hours, the divers had collected more than six thousand Spanish coins and a number of glass and clay containers.

The archaeological detectives

The Western Australian Maritime Museum in Perth was notified and a team of archaeologists was formed to investigate the wreck more closely. Its leader, Graeme Henderson, found himself and his team in such a remote part of the country that he had to set up his headquarters in a sheep-shearing shed. Excavating underwater is much more difficult than land excavation. Henderson set up a grid of ropes over the wreck so that the position of every object could be recorded accurately before it was taken to the surface. Another problem of working underwater is the thick silt and sand that covers the ocean bed. This has to be removed by special airlifts (like large, powerful vacuum cleaners without the bags) so that the timbers and smaller objects could be seen. When the wreck had been cleared, Henderson saw

Restoring a wooden barrel found in the wreck. Barrels like this usually contained salt beef or pork, as fresh meat would not last long onboard ship.

Below Divers airlifting silt from the wreck of the hull. The silt is sucked up a tube and is then spread far away from the wreck.

that he had uncovered a wooden ship, 100 feet long, made of oak and spruce.

Altogether, the divers found 19,000 Spanish coins, dating from 1759 to 1809. This did not necessarily mean that the ship was Spanish, for these coins were an important international currency at that time. Identifying the ship was to be the most difficult job for Henderson and his team.

They found some interesting clues. One was the top of a barrel with the words MESS BEEF BOSTON MASS carved into it. Some copper fittings had the name J. Davies inscribed on them. Eight British guns were found in the wreck. Once again, this was not proof of its origins, because most cannons were produced by Great Britain in those days. By using all the clues and looking at old naval documents, Henderson was able to identify the ship. A shipwright in Bath, Maine, named Jonathan Davies, had built 22 ships between 1785 and 1819, so perhaps the ship was American. The latest coin was dated 1809, fitting in with this period of time.

Above The beef barrel lid that was marked with the words MESS BEEF BOSTON MASS

The mystery was solved when Henderson looked at some insurance documents. The ship was the *Rapid*, which had been sailing from Boston to Canton, China, in 1811 when it was wrecked off Point Cloates. Archaeology and detective work had paid off.

An artist's impression of the *Mary Rose* under sail. Finding the Tudor warship has given us a better idea of what the ship really looked like. Before it was raised, we only had unreliable sixteenth-century drawings.

The King's great loss

When a ship is lost in dark, murky waters, divers often need the help of sophisticated technology. This was certainly true in the case of the *Mary Rose*, the pride of King Henry VIII's navy, which set sail from Portsmouth, England, on July 19, 1545. King Henry himself watched it sail toward a French invasion fleet, its gunports open and its decks and masts packed with seven hundred sailors and soldiers ready for battle. Suddenly, a strong gust of wind made the ship tilt over to starboard. Top-heavy with cannons and people, it tipped over and water poured in through its open gunports. This magnificent vessel disappeared under the water within a few seconds. Only thirty men survived.

More than four hundred years later, a skin diver named David McKee decided he would find the

Right On October 11, 1982, the remains of the *Mary Rose*'s hull were raised from the seabed in one piece on a specially designed cradle. It had been previously lifted underwater and placed on the cradle, which was lined with airbags to protect the delicate timbers of the hull.

Mary Rose. In 1965, he and Margaret Rule, an archaeologist, began using underwater scanners to help locate the wreck in the dark waters. Every time the scanners detected a bulge on the seabed, divers went down to investigate. In 1971, the wreck was finally found under 40 feet of water. It was excavated and recorded before being raised and brought to the shore on October 11, 1982.

Below A bronze muzzle-loading gun, fitted to a carriage that allowed it to be moved for cleaning and reloading. It fired iron shot that could damage enemy rigging, decks, and hulls.

The *Mary Rose* and its contents were an archaeological sensation, for the ship was very well preserved. We now know what the sailors ate from—the officers had pewter plates, while the lower ranks had wooden ones. In their spare time, the men played the board game backgammon, fished, watched cockfights, or played pipes. A case of longbows was raised intact, with more than 3,500 arrows, complete with goose- or swan-feather vanes. The mud of the seabed had hidden the *Mary Rose*, and preserved one side perfectly.

An assortment of items that belonged to sailors aboard the *Mary Rose*, including a comb, a rosary, a pocket sundial, and a whistle. The ship is a true time capsule, preserved almost exactly as it was on the day in 1545 when it sank.

The pride of Hitler's fleet

One of the most spectacular discoveries of modern warfare was the location by Robert Ballard in 1989 of the World War II German battleship Bismarck, lying 15,400 feet below the surface of the Atlantic Ocean. This, the greatest ship in Hitler's fleet, was sunk by the British Royal Navy on May 27, 1941. It is impossible for a human diver to descend so deep underwater, so Ballard developed Argo, a video camera that could be suspended from a ship. He hoped that Argo would be able to locate the ship on the ocean bed using sonar, and then send video pictures back to the control vessel on the surface.

The *Bismarck* was an exceptional ship— 850 feet long and 118 feet wide at its widest point. The eight 15-inch guns were the biggest ever placed on a German battleship.

The Sinking of the Bismarck by C.E. Turner. At 10:36 A.M., already in flames, the ship was hit by a torpedo and sank three minutes later. Out of a crew of over two thousand, only 110 survived.

After two years of searching, the warship was discovered and filmed. The pictures sent back to the control ship were superb, and by studying them, Ballard was able to piece together the ship's last moments. "As I stared at those mute guns and the blasted superstructure, the awful last hours of the Bismarck *were suddenly real, immediate... men had lived on this ship, fought bravely for her during her hopeless final battle, and died."—Robert Ballard's first impressions on seeing the* Bismarck.

After being attacked by British ships, the crippled Bismarck, *on fire and sinking, had rolled over with its hull (bottom) in the air. Its four huge gun turrets, complete with 15-inch guns, had fallen from the deck and plunged to the ocean floor. Once all the air inside had been forced out by seawater, the ship rolled upright and glided downward. It landed heavily on the slope of an extinct underwater volcano, causing a landslide that carried it another half-mile deeper. This has been the* Bismarck's *resting place ever since, almost 2 miles away from where she sank.*

Robert Ballard sees the deep ocean floor as a huge museum of the hidden past that has never been open to visits from the public. He has already opened it again by filming the wreck of the ill-fated ocean liner Titanic, *and he hopes to continue by finding and visiting other shipwrecks.*

Robert Ballard in the Argo control room (**right**) and a video image of one of the *Bismarck's* gun mounts (**above**)

TIME LINE

A.D. 0   950   1900

c. 100,000–40,000 B.C.

Neanderthals alive;
Shanidar Cave in
Iraq occupied

PRFCTFCTVS*CFSQVFI*
IN PACE *VIXIT ANNIS VIIII
MENSES VIIII DIES III
NVTRICATVS DEO CRISTO MARTVRIBVS

1941

German battleship
Bismarck sunk in
Atlantic Ocean

c. 13,000 B.C.

Cave paintings
made at Lascaux,
France

A.D. 250

Construction of
catacombs begins
in Rome

1542

Spanish invaders
begin destruc-
tion of Mayan
civilization

c. 1300 B.C.

Ice Man dies in
Otztal Alps in
what is now
Austria

c. 700

First towns
in North
America
built in middle
Mississippi Valley

1545

King Henry VIII
of England's
flagship, *Mary
Rose,* sinks

1974

Discovery of terracotta
army of Qin Shi
Huang Di in China

c. 500 B.C.

Rise of Indus Valley
civilization in what
is now Pakistan.
Beginnings of town
planning

1811

Merchant ship
Rapid wrecked
off west coast
of Australia

1989

Wreck of battleship
Bismarck found by
American
oceanographer
Robert Ballard

c. 250 B.C.

Mayan civilization
established in
Central America

1839–42

Ruins of Mayan
cities discovered
by John Lloyd
Stephens and
Frederick
Catherwood

1860s

Building of under-
ground sewer
system in London,
England

1991

Preserved body of
the Ice Man found
in the Austrian
Alps

GLOSSARY

Afterlife According to many religions, the place where the souls of people go after death.

Archaeologist A person who discovers and studies artifacts, buildings, and other objects from the past.

Battleship A heavily armed fighting ship.

Catacombs Underground tunnels and chambers where bodies are buried.

Dredger A machine used to remove mud and other material from a riverbed.

Excavate To dig up.

Hieroglyphic Writing that consists of pictures rather than letters.

Incense A substance that is burned to give off a fragrant smoke.

Jade A green, semiprecious stone that is often used in ornamental carvings.

Neanderthals Early people who lived in Europe and southwest Asia between 250,000 and 30,000 years ago.

Obsidian A dark, glassy type of rock that is produced during volcanic eruptions.

Peat A brownish, mudlike substance formed from decayed organic matter.

Radiocarbon dating A technique used to discover the age of an artifact by measuring how much of a type of carbon it contains.

Salvage To rescue lost ships or other property.

Vanes Feathers attached to an arrow to make it fly straight.

Yucatán The broad peninsula that forms the northeastern part of Mexico and parts of Guatemala and Belize.

FURTHER INFORMATION

BOOKS

Cork, Barbara and Struan Reid. *Archaeology*. Tulsa, OK: EDC Press, 1985.

Frazee, Charles and Halie Kay Yopp. *Early People and the First Civilizations*. New York: Delos Publications, 1990.

Guisso, R. *The First Emperor of China*. New York: Carol Publishing Group, 1989.

Hicks, Peter. *Pompeii and Herculaneum*. Digging Up the Past. New York: Thomson Learning, 1996.

Hicks, Peter. *Troy and Knossos*. Digging up the Past. Austin, TX: Raintree Steck-Vaughn, 1996.

McIntosh, Jane. *Archeology*. Eyewitness Books. New York: Alfred A. Knopf, 1991.

Putnam, Jim. *Mummy*. Eyewitness Books. New York: Alfred A. Knopf, 1993.

INDEX

afterlife 11, 13, 18
Almendariz, Ricardo 21
Alps, Otztal 4, 46
Animals 4, 8, 18, 26, 29–30
archaeologists 4, 6, 8, 10, 13,
    19, 24, 26, 29, 40, 43
archaeology 6, 20, 23–24, 42, 44
Argo 44–5
armor 6, 12–13, 36
Australia 39, 46
Austria 4, 46

Ballard, Robert 44–46
Bazalgette, Joseph 32–33
Bismarck 7, 44–46
bison 8, 29
bodies 4–5, 9, 11, 15, 26, 28, 46
bones 2, 6, 16–17, 19, 25
bronze 5–7, 10, 12–13, 43
buildings 4, 16, 20–22
burials 4, 6, 9, 11–15, 18–19

Cagoules 35–36
Cahokia 18–19
Canada 8
catacombs 14–17, 35–37, 46
Catherwood, Frederick 21–23, 46
caves 3, 26–29, 46
cemeteries 14–17
Central America 7, 20–21, 23, 46
charnel houses 19
Chichén Itzá 21, 23–25
China 9, 13, 39, 42, 46
cities 3, 7, 14–16, 20–22, 24,
    30–35, 37–38, 46
coins 6, 39–41
Communards 17
Copán 21–22

dating 5, 7, 41
Deloncle, Eugène 35
disease 7, 19, 30, 32, 35
Dou Wan 9–11
drains 30, 31, 34

farmers 4, 12
flint 5–6, 25, 28, 30
food 18, 29, 38
fossores 14
France 29, 36, 46

Great Britain 21, 32–33, 41

Head-Smashed-In, Buffalo
    Jump, Canada 8
Henry VIII, King of England
    42, 46
Hitler, Adolf 7, 44
hunter-gatherers 30
hunting 8, 29–30

Ice Man 4–5
Iran 27
Iraq 26–27, 46
iron 7, 9–10, 43
Italy 2, 14

jade 10–11, 25

KGB 38

Lascaux, France 29–30, 46
Liu Sheng 9–11
London, England 30, 32, 34,
    35, 37, 46

mammoths 8
Mayans 7, 20–21, 23–25, 46
McKee, David 42
Mexico 20–21
Mississippi temple-mounds
    18–19
Mohenjo-daro 30–31
mummies 15

Native Americans 8
Neanderthals 26–28, 46
North America 8, 18, 46
Olsen-Chubbuck, Colorado 8

Palenque 21–23
Palermo, Sicily 15
Paris, France 16–17, 35–36
pottery 12, 40
pyramids 22–23

Rapid 42, 46
Rome, Italy 14–16, 46

sacrifices 20, 24, 25
sewers 30, 32–35, 37, 46
Shanidar Cave, Iraq 26–27, 46
Shi Huang Di, Emperor of
    China 12–13, 46
ships 7, 39–42, 44–46
shipwrecks 3, 39, 45
skeletons 17, 27–28
Solecki, Ralph 26–27
Southern Cult 19
Soviet Union 38
Stephens, John Lloyd 21–24, 46

temples 18, 20, 22–23, 25
terra cotta army 12–13
Thiers, Louis Adolphe 17
Thompson, Edward 24–25
Tikal 21
tombs 10–13
tunnels 3, 26, 30, 32–34, 37–38

United States 8, 18–19, 33, 38,
    41–42
Uxmal 20–21, 23

weapons 6, 7, 25, 35, 43,
    44–5
Wu-ti 9

Yu-xia 11
Yucatán peninsula, Mexico 20–23

Zagros Mountains, Iraq 26–27